Padraig Coyle was born in D
Patrick's College, Armagh,
Trinity College Dublin, wh
sportsman and Gaelic foot
presenter and journalist for L
before turning freelance in 1986. He is a regular sports broadcaster on BBC radio and writes on sport in Ireland for the *Independent*, the *Observer*, the *Irish News*, the *Sunday Life* and the *Sunday Tribune*. He also contributes regularly to publications in the United States, Australia and on the Continent.

The GAELIC GAMES Quiz Book

PADRAIG COYLE

THE
BLACKSTAFF
PRESS

BELFAST

First published in 1989 by
The Blackstaff Press Limited
3 Galway Park, Dundonald, Belfast BT16 0AN, Northern Ireland

© Padraig Coyle, 1989
All rights reserved

Printed by The Guernsey Press Company Limited

British Library Cataloguing in Publication Data
Coyle, Padraig
The Gaelic games quiz book.
1. Gaelic sports
I. Title
796

ISBN 0-85640-429-2

CONTENTS

Questions

General Knowledge 1	3
General Knowledge 2	4
General Knowledge 3	5
International Rules Football	7
Hurling 1	8
General Knowledge 4	9
Football 1	10
County Colours	13
General Knowledge 5	14
General Knowledge 6	15
Clubs and Counties 1	16
General Knowledge 7	17
Footballers and Counties	19
Hurlers and Counties	20
Clubs and Counties 2	22
Brothers	23
Football 2	24
Hurling 2	26
Football 3	27
General Knowledge 8	28
Referees do have Homes!	29
General Knowledge 9	30
Minor Gaelic Games	32
General Knowledge 10	34
Football 4	35
Footballers and Clubs – Tyrone	36
Footballers and Clubs – Monaghan	37
Footballers and Clubs – Mayo	38

Footballers and Clubs – Cork	39
Footballers and Clubs – Meath	40
General Knowledge 11	42
General Knowledge 12	43
General Knowledge 13	44
Minor Football	45
Camogie	47
General Knowledge 14	48
Hurlers and Clubs – Galway	49
Hurlers and Clubs – Cork	50
London Calling	52
General Knowledge 15	53
Name the Grounds	55
Scribes and Commentators	56
Referees of Yore	57
Who Am I?	58
Women Play Football Too	61
The American Scene	62
Name the Boss	64
True or False?	65
Handball	66
General Knowledge 16	67
Answers	73

NOTE

Sport, whatever form it takes, is meant to be enjoyed, not endured. Compiling the questions for this Gaelic games quiz book has been a labour of love, bringing back memories of names and occasions that made the sporting headlines in their days.

The questions vary in degrees of difficulty – some are easy, others are hard. But someone, somewhere, will know the answers. Take on the challenge – that is the point of it all, whether under or over the bar.

Whilst every effort has been taken to ensure the accuracy of the information in this book, the compiler and the publisher cannot accept responsibility for any errors.

Questions in this book incorporate events to the end of May 1989.

Sincere thanks to P.J. McKeefry, sports editor of the *Irish News* for the use of photographs, to Michael McGeary of *Sunday Life* for reading the proofs, and to all those journalists and nameless people who have reported games and written programmes since the GAA was formed.

To the players
who provided the facts and to the
journalists who recorded them

To Jane and the kids
for waiting patiently for the full-time whistle

To my brothers and brother-in-law
for their constructive suggestions

And to my late father,
who introduced me to sport, took me to matches,
watched me play and taught me to forgive
referees – eventually

Questions

General Knowledge 1

Answers on page 73

1. Which county has won the greatest number of All-Ireland senior hurling titles?
2. How many times?
3. When did Tipperary win their first All-Ireland senior hurling title?
4. Who once left the Sam Maguire Cup in the dressing room at Croke Park?
5. Name the Dublin player who transferred sports to Manchester United in the late 1970s.
6. Which is the only county outside of Ireland to hold the All-Ireland hurling crown?
7. Name the year in which they won.
8. Who is the Wicklow man who played for Kildare, went to New York and came back to play for Cork?
9. Who led Galway to their first National Hurling League title?
10. Name the 1987 Ulster senior provincial football champions.
11. Who were the beaten finalists in the 1987 All-Ireland senior hurling final?
12. Who was Tyrone's penalty-taker in the 1986 All-Ireland final against Kerry?
13. Who is the footballer who played in a National League final and an FAI cup final in successive weeks?
14. Which county is credited with perfecting the hand-pass in the 1970s?
15. Name the last Ulster county to win the All-Ireland senior football title.

16 Who is the Derry player who emigrated to Australian Rules in 1988?
17 Why was the 1984 All-Ireland hurling final played in Thurles?
18 Where was the first leg of the 1989 National Football League final staged?
19 One player was sent off in the 1988 Cork v. Meath replay. Who was he?
20 When were the All-Star awards introduced?

General Knowledge 2

Answers on page 74

21 In 1960 which referee took charge of both the football and hurling senior All-Ireland finals?
22 In the winning Dublin hurling team of 1927, how many players were native to the county?
23 In the hurling final of 1901, when London beat Cork, were all the players on the winning side Londoners?
24 In that final, how many players were there on each side?
25 Cork and London met again in the 1902 decider. What was remarkable about London's performance?
26 Who captained Tyrone to the 1986 All-Ireland football final?
27 Which club side has Jack O'Shea played for in the later part of his career?
28 With which club would you associate Mikey Sheehy and Ger Power?
29 What colour are the flags used to indicate goals and points?

30 Name the goalkeeper who won a record seven senior All-Ireland football medals between 1931 and 1946.

31 What is the largest official attendance recorded for an All-Ireland football final – (a) 90,556; (b) 93,271 or (c) 95,100?

32 Name the year and the teams.

33 When did Christy Ring die?

34 When Cork's hurlers defeated Wexford in the 1954 All-Ireland final, Ring established the record for senior medals. How many had he won?

35 Another player equalled that record in 1965. Who was he?

36 Which county won the All-Ireland senior football title in 1968?

37 Who was the top scorer that year in the championship?

38 Name the Ulster player who was the leading scorer in the 1986 senior football championship?

39 When was the first 80-minute All-Ireland senior football final?

40 Who were the finalists?

General Knowledge 3

Answers on page 75

41 When was the first 70-minute All-Ireland senior football final?

42 Who were the finalists?

43 Which two Ulster counties reached the 1985 National Football League final?

44 Apart from 1988, when was the last All-Ireland football final that ended in a draw?

45 Who were the eventual winners?
46 When did Monaghan make their All-Ireland football debut?
47 Which county has a red hand for its crest?
48 Who were the first Ulster team to win the Sam Maguire Cup?
49 In which year was the Sam Maguire trophy first played for?
50 Who were the winners in that year?
51 Who were the first winners of the Sam Óg Maguire Cup?
52 Armagh have played in two All-Ireland senior football finals. When?
53 The 1950 football champions won again in 1951. Who were they?
54 Name the three Spillane brothers in the Kerry teams of the 1980s.
55 Who is the youngest brother?
56 Who was the star of the 1984 Ulster senior football final, and why?
57 Name the man more usually associated with boxing and horses who won a minor football medal in 1948.
58 Why was the 1987 Leinster hurling final between Offaly and Kilkenny postponed?
59 Monaghan won the 1985 National Football League final having previously faced a replay in the semi-final. Who were their opponents and where did they play?
60 Maradonna's 'hand of God' helped Argentina to beat England in the World Cup finals in Mexico. Who had a 'hand' in the winning goal for Offaly in the replay of the 1972 All-Ireland football final?

International Rules Football

Answers on page 76

61 Name the Australian coach on the 1987 tour of Ireland.
62 How long did the International Rules matches last?
63 How much was a goal worth?
64 How much was an 'over' worth?
65 What term described 1 point?
66 Who was the Irish referee during the 1987 series?
67 Name the managers of the Irish teams in 1986 and 1987.
68 What shape was the ball used in the 1987 test series?
69 Name the respective captains in the 1987 test series.
70 Who was the Aussies' coach when they came to Ireland in 1984?
71 Which club did Australia's Robert Dipierdomencio play for in 1984?
72 Name the other years when there have been encounters with the Aussies.
73 What was different about the series in the 1960s?
74 Who were the first holders of the International Cup?
75 What might the Australians have been suffering from?
76 How did Meath fare in Australia in 1968?
77 On what trophy would you find the inscription 'Paddy Hann's gold, Kalgoorlie'?
78 Beitzel was a radio commentator and editor of a sports magazine. What was the magazine called?
79 Which club did Steve Malaxos play for in 1984?
80 Who captained the Aussies on their first trip to Ireland in 1967?

Hurling 1

Answers on page 77

81 Who captained the Cork hurlers in centenary year?

82 Which club did he win a county medal with in the 1983 championship?

83 In 1987 who said, 'The famine is over, you ain't seen nothing yet'?

84 Cork had two dual stars playing in that final against Tipperary. Who were they?

85 What is the Poc Fada?

86 Where is it staged?

87 Up to 1988, who was the All-Ireland Poc Fada champion?

88 When did Galway win their first All-Ireland senior hurling crown?

89 When was the next time?

90 Who coached the Galway team in that year?

91 What is the name of the All-Ireland hurling trophy?

92 Which teams contested the first All-Ireland final in 1887?

93 Who were alleged to have been stricken by a 'priest's curse'?

94 In which year did Offaly win the Leinster hurling title for the first time?

95 Which two counties took the All-Ireland senior hurling championship at their first attempt?

96 Who was the Cork manager when they were defeated by Kilkenny in the 1983 All-Ireland senior hurling final?

97 Who were the first Ulster club to take the All-Ireland hurling title and when did they achieve it?

98 Whom did they beat in the final?

99 Who was the oldest player on the Wexford hurling team that defeated Kilkenny in a Leinster semi-final in 1984?

100 Who played on even though he had punctured a lung during a Munster hurling semi-final in 1984?

General Knowledge 4

Answers on page 78

101 Which county is credited with developing the hand-pass in the 1920s?

102 Former Taoiseach, Jack Lynch, won six All-Ireland medals in successive years. How many were for hurling?

103 Which was the first county to achieve four-in-a-row All-Ireland football titles?

104 When did Kerry achieve their first four-in-a-row All-Ireland football titles?

105 In 1967 Galway were bidding for their fifth successive football final? Who stopped them?

106 Who halted Kerry's bid for five-in-a-row football finals in 1933?

107 Liverpool goalkeeper Bruce Grobbelaar is renowned for his antics and gymnastics during matches. Which 1930s Kerry goalkeeper acted similarly?

108 The 1988 hurling final marked a musical first for the Artane Boys' Band. Why?

109 Who has the nickname 'Bomber'?
110 When did Congress reduce the number of outfield players from 17 to 15?
111 Who begged for 'five minutes more' and why?
112 Who was playing and where was the final being held?
113 Name the first captain to hold the Sam Maguire Cup.
114 In Gaelic football what occasion became known as 'Bloody Sunday'?
115 How many people were killed?
116 Who was the player?
117 How was he honoured?
118 Monaghan almost won the 1930 All-Ireland senior final without a ball being kicked. Why?
119 Which county won six successive National Football League titles?
120 In which years?

Football 1

Answers on page 79

121 What record did Mayo set between August 1935 and August 1937?
122 In the 1931 All-Ireland semi-final against Kerry, Mayo's Paddy Moclair had a goal disallowed. Why?
123 In the 1930s who was nicknamed 'the Boy Wonder of Football'?
124 What age was he when he made his senior championship debut?
125 When was the Cusack Stand opened?

126 What was exceptional about the Laois team that were beaten by Mayo in the 1936 All-Ireland senior final?

127 Paddy Boylan thought he had scored the winning point for Cavan in the 1927 senior football final against Kerry. What did the referee decide?

128 Which Kerry forward of the 1940s was nicknamed 'Gega'?

129 When and where did he make his debut?

130 One of the 1934 All-Ireland semi-finals played the equivalent of three halves. Which one was it?

131 Where was it played and why did it last so long?

132 The result was 1–8 to 0–8. In favour of whom, and did it stand?

133 How many substitutes did Kerry use in the last few minutes of the 1938 All-Ireland replay with Galway?

134 Why?

135 In which year was the rotational system for All-Ireland semi-finals introduced?

136 The 1941 Leinster football final was played after the All-Ireland semi-final. What was the reason?

137 Which player almost missed the 1945 All-Ireland football final?

138 Who captained Antrim to the Ulster championship and All-Ireland semi-final of 1946?

139 Cavan beat Kerry at the Polo Grounds, New York, in the 1947 All-Ireland football final. What was the score?

140 What was 'Gunner' Brady's first name?

Kilkenny's Ger Henderson out on his own in the All-Ireland hurling final against Cork in 1982

County Colours

Answers on page 80

What colours do these counties play in?

141 Kildare
142 Antrim
143 Cavan
144 Fermanagh
145 Derry
146 Leitrim
147 Down
148 Clare
149 Longford
150 Carlow
151 Galway
152 Kerry
153 Donegal
154 Kilkenny
155 Roscommon
156 Sligo
157 Limerick
158 Westmeath
159 Laois
160 Louth

General Knowledge 5

Answers on page 82

161 The 1987 National Football League quarter-final between Dublin and Cork ended in a draw. What happened next?

162 Then what happened?

163 Who is the present public relations officer for the GAA?

164 Which former Armagh football and hurling ace emigrated to Australia in 1988?

165 What football club did he play with?

166 Who was the first camogie player to win All-Ireland club medals with different teams in different provinces?

167 Name the clubs.

168 Who were the winners of the National Hurling League final in 1989?

169 Who did they beat and what was the score?

170 Outside of London where is there a Hyde Park?

171 Dick Curtis won four All-Ireland football medals with Dublin in the 1890s. What was his other sporting pastime?

172 What was the score in the 1989 Dr McKenna Cup final?

173 Where was the game played?

174 Which player scored a hat trick of goals?

175 There was a minute's silence before the game. Why?

176 When was Gaelic football and hurling first played at Wembley Stadium, London?

177 Which teams were involved?

178 When did the experiment end?
179 In which year did the All-Stars appear at Wembley?
180 Who were their hurling and football opponents?

General Knowledge 6

Answers on page 83

181 In the 1949 Munster hurling final Cork and Tipperary went to a replay and extra time. Before extra time was played, Cork rested on the field. What did Tipperary do?
182 Did this have any benefit?
183 Which Cork hurler–footballer bowed out after the 1986 hurling final against Galway?
184 Which club team did he play for?
185 In which county is Ballycastle Hurling Club?
186 The 1989 Cork captain played soccer for Cork Hibernians in the 1970s. Who is he?
187 Name the Ulster hurler who was injured when playing soccer against Glentoran in the 1989 Bass Irish Cup.
188 Offaly took their first All-Ireland senior football title in 1971. Name their captain.
189 In which county is Camross Hurling Club?
190 In which county would you find the hurling side, Patrickswell?
191 St Martin's Hurling Club is in which county?
192 Where is Gort Hurling Club?
193 In which county would you find Lacken Gaelic Football Club?

194 What was the score in the 1988 All-Ireland minor football final?

195 Name the winners of the first Munster football title in 1888.

196 Up to 1988, how many Munster senior football titles have Kerry won – (a) 31–40; (b) 41–50; (c) 51–60 or (d) 61–70?

197 It took three matches to decide the 1899 Munster football championship final between Cork and Tipperary. What happened in the first match?

198 What happened in the second match?

199 Who were the eventual winners in the third match?

200 In 1989 which footballer was ruled ineligible to play for New York against Cork because he played for Westmeath?

Clubs and Counties 1

Answers on page 84

In which counties would you find the following football clubs:

201 Nemo Rangers
202 Bellaghy
203 Clann na Gael (Ulster)
204 St Vincent's
205 St Grellan's
206 Clann na Gael (Connacht)
207 Ardboe
208 UCD
209 Bryansford

210 Casements
211 Castleisland Desmonds
212 Scotstown
213 Cooley Kickams
214 Garrymore
215 Thomond College
216 Headford
217 Lamh Dearg
218 Clontibret
219 Ballyhegan
220 St Faithleach's

General Knowledge 7

Answers on page 85

221 Who were the beaten finalists in the 1986 All-Ireland club hurling final?
222 Name the Clare hurler sent off in the 1987 Munster championship game with Tipperary.
223 When Tipperary won the 1987 Munster senior hurling championship, it ended a gap of how many years?
224 Who was the Tipperary coach in 1987?
225 What did the 1939 All-Ireland hurling final become known as?
226 Why?
227 Name the counties in that 1939 final.
228 In the 1984 Cork v. Tipperary Munster hurling final, who was the one survivor from the Tipperary team beaten by Limerick in 1973?

229 Who captained Tipperary in that 1984 Munster hurling final?
230 Cork and Tipperary drew in the 1987 Munster senior hurling final. Why was the replay staged in Killarney?
231 According to a well-known local saying, what was saved when Cork were 'beat'?
232 Which county achieved the hurling treble in 1964 and 1965?
233 What are Babs Keating's five S's?
234 Tipperary's fund-raising drive of 1987 included an unusual raffle. What was the prize?
235 Which Republic of Ireland footballer's father was a hurler for Tipperary?
236 Who was the Ulster hurler named as a 1988 All-Star replacement?
237 Which club does he play for?
238 Which club side were the All-Ireland club champions in hurling in 1987?
239 On their way to the title, whom did they defeat in the provincial final, the All-Ireland semi-final, and the final?
240 Who were the winners of the 1986 All-Ireland club hurling final?

Footballers and Counties

Answers on page 86

With which counties would you associate the following footballers?

241 Barry Brennan
242 Joe Kernan
243 Peter McGinnity
244 Iggy Jones
245 Peter Rooney
246 Ollie Brady
247 Eugene Sherry
248 Martin McHugh
249 Plunkett Donaghy
250 Brian McGilligan
251 Liam Currams
252 T.J. Kilgallon
253 Tommy Drumm
254 Eddie Boyle
255 Colm O'Rourke
256 Willie Brennan
257 Kevin Kehily
258 Danny Murray
259 Mickey Kearins
260 John Egan

Hurlers and Counties

Answers on page 87

With which counties would you associate the following hurlers?

261 Aiden Fogarty
262 Donal Armstrong
263 Denis Kilcoyne
264 P.J. Cuddy
265 Leonard Enwright
266 Jimmy Smith
267 Richie Power
268 Mick Jacob
269 Nicky English
270 Joe Cooney
271 Martin Bailie
272 Thomas Moylan
273 Ciaran Barr
274 Ollie Kilkenny
275 John Corvan
276 Noel Skehan
277 Jimmy Carlisle
278 Mick Mackey
279 Eddie Keher
280 John Fenton

Offaly launch an attack on the Kerry goalmouth in the 1981 All-Ireland football final.

Clubs and Counties 2

Answers on page 88

In which counties would you find the following hurling clubs?

281 St Rynagh's
282 Blackrock
283 Rathnure
284 Glen Rovers
285 The Fenians
286 St Finbarr's
287 O'Donovan Rossas
288 James Stephens
289 Ballyhale Shamrocks
290 Castlegar
291 Ballycran
292 Mount Sion
293 Ballygalget
294 Lavey
295 Cuchulainns
296 Borris-Ileigh
297 Portaferry
298 Loughgiel Shamrocks
299 Kilruane McDonaghs
300 Buffers Alley

Brothers

Answers on page 89

301 The Laois team that lost to Mayo in the 1936 All-Ireland senior football final featured six players with the surname Delaney. How many of them were related?

302 What was the relationship?

303 Their names were Bill, Chris, Jack, Tom and Mick. Who was the uncle?

304 Name the three brothers who played for Galway in the 1980 hurling final against Limerick.

305 Name the brothers who played on the Wexford team in the 1951, 1954, 1955, and 1956 hurling finals.

306 There were four brothers on the Kilkenny hurling team that played against Galway in the 1987 All-Ireland final. Who were they?

307 There were four brothers on the Kilkenny hurling team that played against Cork in the 1970 All-Ireland final. Who were they?

308 When was the first time that three brothers started and finished on a winning All-Ireland senior team?

309 Name the brothers.

310 Which club did they play with?

311 What connection did their father have with the team?

312 Name the brothers who played for Kerry in the 1932 football final against Mayo.

313 What is the surname of the famous footballing brothers from Templenoe?

314 Who are the hurling brothers who played for Cork in the 1986 All-Ireland senior and minor finals?

23

315 Three brothers played on the winning Wexford hurling team that defeated Cork in the 1893 final. Who were they?

316 Name the brothers who played football for Kerry during the 1960s – one of them played for London in the 1969 All-Ireland junior final.

317 In the 1930s with which county would you have associated John Joe and Tom O'Reilly?

318 In 1982 two brothers from Offaly were given All-Star awards. Who were they?

319 Name the three brothers who have represented Burren in Ulster and All-Ireland club football finals.

320 Name the footballing family who played for Clann na Gael in the 1987 All-Ireland club football final against St Finbarr's.

Football 2

Answers on page 90

321 When did Ulster first win the Railway Cup in football?

322 Who led Ulster to victory over Leinster in the 1947 Railway Cup?

323 Which county had the strongest representation on that 1947 Ulster team?

324 Which counties were not represented on the Ulster team?

325 Which is the 'Royal' county?

326 When did the 'Royal' county first win an All-Ireland senior football title?

327 In the Leinster championship match against Kildare in

1949, only 13 Meath players took part in the pre-match parade. Who was missing and why?

328 Who captained Meath?
329 Which Armagh player missed a penalty in the 1953 senior football final at Croke Park?
330 What was the offence that led to the penalty decision?
331 Armagh were defeated in this final. By whom?
332 Whom did Armagh beat in the Ulster final that year, and where was the game played?
333 In the 1953 National Football League final against Cavan, the Dublin goalkeeper Tony O'Grady was the odd one out. Why?
334 In the 1955 All-Ireland senior final between Dublin and Kerry, what was Kerry fullback Jerome O'Shea's achievement?
335 Who was the Cahirciveen man on the Kerry team that drew with Kildare in the 1926 final and missed the replay because of illness?
336 Name the player on the Dublin team in the 1958 football final who went on to become their manager in the 1970s.
337 In which city would you now find the original Hogan Stand?
338 Who was locked out of the 1957 Louth v. Cork All-Ireland senior football final?
339 Apart from a football team, what else did he lead?
340 What was his first number one record?

Hurling 2

Answers on page 92

341 Name the great Offaly hurler who received an All-Ireland winners' medal in 1985 even though he was too ill to play in the final.

342 Name Cork's All-Ireland hurling captain in their 1986 win against Galway.

343 Who was Kilkenny's manager when they were defeated by Galway in the 1987 final?

344 What colours do Cork's hurlers play in?

345 What are Tipperary's colours?

346 What are Waterford's colours?

347 What are Wexford's colours?

348 Who was Tipperary's goalkeeper in the 1989 National Hurling League final?

349 He made his county debut in 1987. Against whom?

350 Which county does George O'Connor play for?

351 In 1988 who did Antrim beat to gain promotion for the first time to Division One of the National Hurling League?

352 The 1984 All-Time All-Star award was given to a hurling star of the late 1930s and 1940s. Who was he and what was his county?

353 He captained Kilkenny in an All-Ireland final. When, against whom and did they win?

354 In the 1986 All-Ireland final Cork defeated Galway 4–13 to 2–15. Who scored Cork's vital last goal?

355 When were Galway given permission to play in the Munster provincial championship?

356 How long did they stay there before returning to Connacht?
357 In the 1980s which county did Eugene Coughlan play for?
358 Who were the 1988 Ulster club hurling champions?
359 Whom did they beat in the final?
360 Who were the captains of the Tipperary and Cork teams in the 1987 Munster final?

Football 3

Answers on page 93

361 Who scored the winning goal for Louth in the 1957 All-Ireland football final against Cork?
362 Down beat Kerry in the 1960 final, but against whom did they retain the All-Ireland in 1961?
363 In the game against Kerry in 1960, Jim McCartan kicked the ball, but who dropped it for Down's first goal?
364 Minutes later, Down were awarded a penalty. Who scored?
365 In what years did Galway achieve their hat trick of All-Ireland senior titles?
366 How many goals did Galway goalkeeper Johnny Geraghty concede in the three finals?
367 Enda Colleran captained Galway in 1965 and 1966. Who led them in 1964?
368 Which Dublin player was nicknamed 'the Blue Panther'?
369 How many Munster football finals did Kerry play in between 1975 and 1987?

370 How many of the finals did they win in successive seasons?

371 Who captained Kerry in 1984 – football's centenary year?

372 Name his club team at the time.

373 What means of transport would Kerry's Mick O'Connell and Ger Lynch have used to travel to training sessions?

374 Why?

375 When was the first All-Ireland final played at Croke Park?

376 The result of the 1891 final – played in February 1892 – between Dublin (Young Irelands) and Cork (Clondrohid) was 2–1 to 1–9. Who were the winners?

377 In the 1894 final – played in 1895 – the score was Dublin 0–6, Cork 1–1. What was the outcome?

378 Who has received the greatest number of Texaco Footballer of the Year awards?

379 How many times?

380 Name the years.

General Knowledge 8

Answers on page 94

381 Who was the first president of the GAA?

382 Who presided over the GAA in centenary year?

383 Who was the first Ulsterman to become president of the GAA?

384 What has been the longest period of time between elections of GAA presidents?

385 How many Ulstermen have been GAA presidents?
386 Who are they?
387 Where is Semple Stadium?
388 In which city is Jones Road?
389 Name the main GAA ground in Killarney.
390 When was the first Texaco Footballer of the Year award made?
391 Who received it?
392 How many other Ulster footballers have been honoured this way?
393 Who are they and when did they receive their awards?
394 One manager–coach has been awarded the title. Who is he?
395 Who was the first Texaco Hurler of the Year?
396 Where and when was the GAA founded?
397 Who is Croke Park named after?
398 Who is the Cusack Stand at Croke Park named after?
399 When did Offaly win their first All-Ireland senior hurling title?
400 Whom did they beat in the final?

Referees do have Homes!

Answers on page 95

With which counties would you associate the following referees?

401 Michael Cranny
402 Seamus Alderidge

403 John Gough
404 Mickey Kearins
405 Pascal Long
406 Michael Quinn
407 Joe Kearney
408 Tommy Sugrue
409 Anthony O'Neill
410 Pat Russell
411 Pat Delaney
412 Gerry McClory
413 Tommy Howard
414 Paddy Collins
415 Michael O'Sullivan
416 John Moore
417 Michael Donnellan
418 Willie Horgan
419 Maurice Ferguson
420 Paddy Kavanagh

General Knowledge 9

Answers on page 96

421 Who won the Sigerson Cup in 1988?
422 Who were the winners of the 1989 Sigerson Cup?
423 Whom did they defeat in the final and what was the score?
424 Name the All-Star who played on the University College Cork side?

Kerry's Jack O'Shea and Ger Power too late to stop a shot from Tyrone's Mickey McClure in the 1986 All-Ireland senior football final.

425 Who won the Sigerson Shield in 1989?
426 Who were the beaten finalists and what was the score?
427 Who were the beaten semi-finalists in the 1989 Sigerson Cup?
428 Who were the finalists in the 1989 McRory Cup?
429 Who were the winners?
430 Which former Derry player coaches St Patrick's?
431 Who were the finalists in the 1988 McRory Cup?
432 Who were the winners?
433 What is the name of the All-Ireland trophy they went on to win?
434 Name the RTE commentator who trains the Dublin-based Kerry senior footballers.
435 Name the manager who took Antrim into the National Football League play-offs in 1989.
436 Name the manager who took Cavan out of Division Two of the National Football League in 1989.
437 Name the president of the Ulster Council of the GAA who retired in 1989.
438 Who was elected to succeed him?
439 Who was not elected?
440 Which county won the Dr McKenna Cup in 1988?

Minor Gaelic Games

Answers on page 97

441 Who were the winners of the first All-Ireland minor football title?
442 When was that first All-Ireland minor final?

443 Which county was awarded the title without playing for it?
444 Up to 1988, how many counties have won the title?
445 Up to 1988, which county had won the greatest number of minor football titles?
446 Up to 1988, how often has the minor football final ended in a draw?
447 When did this happen and who were the teams?
448 Who won the replay?
449 How many Ulster counties have won the title?
450 Which counties are they?
451 Name another Ulster county that reached the final, but lost.
452 Which has been the most successful county in Munster minor football?
453 Which county was beaten in three successive All-Ireland minor football finals?
454 Name the years.
455 How many finals have Armagh played in?
456 Name the years.
457 Whom did they beat in 1949?
458 Name the winners of the first Leinster minor football title in 1929.
459 Whom did they beat?
460 Have they ever won the title since then?

General Knowledge 10

Answers on page 98

461 Name the Dublin left full-forward in the 1958 football final.
462 What badge do Dublin have on their jerseys?
463 What is 'Ogie' Moran's first name?
464 Where would you find Liberty Square?
465 Where were the Polo Grounds?
466 Which GAA ground would you be approaching if you left the M1 and travelled along Kennedy Way?
467 What is the name of the venue where the Ulster provincial football finals are usually staged?
468 Where is Pairc Uí Chaoimh?
469 Which teams reached the 1988 Munster club hurling championship final?
470 Who won?
471 Who were the 1988 Leinster club hurling finalists?
472 Which Ulster hurler was made an All-Star in 1989?
473 Which club does he play for?
474 Between 1975 and 1988 Kerry played in 10 All-Ireland senior football finals. How many did they lose?
475 When was the last occasion that both All-Ireland football semi-finals ended in a draw?
476 Which counties were involved?
477 In Higher Education football, who are the holders of the 1989 Ryan Cup?
478 There was a play-off for the title – against whom?
479 Where was it played?
480 With which county do you associate footballer Michael Magee?

Football 4

Answers on page 99

481 Which county has won the greatest number of Connacht senior football titles?

482 Up to 1988, how many provincial titles had they won?

483 When did Roscommon win their first senior provincial title?

484 In which years did Roscommon achieve their senior provincial four-in-a-row?

485 The lowest-scoring Connacht final was in 1912, when Roscommon met Galway. What was the score?

486 When did Sligo last win the Connacht senior title?

487 Which county has yet to win an Ulster senior football title?

488 When Monaghan became Ulster champions in 1979, it ended a gap of how many years?

489 When was the first Ulster championship staged, and who were the winners?

490 When did Armagh collect their first Ulster senior football title?

491 Cavan are the most successful county to come out of Ulster. Up to 1988, when did they last win the provincial crown?

492 Name the last Ulster county to retain their title.

493 Who were the first winners of the Leinster championship?

494 Carlow have won the Leinster title only once. When was that?

495 Whom did they beat?

496 When did Wexford win the last of their nine Leinster football titles?

497 Meath took their first Leinster crown in 1895. When was their next win?

498 Longford have twice reached the Leinster final. Name the years.

499 Who were their opponents in both years and what were the outcomes?

500 Up to 1988, how many Leinster titles had Dublin taken?

Footballers and Clubs – Tyrone

Answers on page 100

With which clubs would you associate the following Tyrone footballers?

501 Aidan Skelton
502 Sean Donnelly
503 Ray Munroe
504 John Lynch
505 Ciaran McGarvey
506 Plunkett Donaghy
507 Kevin McCabe
508 Pauge Quinn
509 Eugene McKenna
510 Paddy Ball
511 Patsy Kerlin
512 Enda Kilpatrick

513 Finbar McConnell
514 Damian O'Hagan
515 Stephen Conway
516 Sean McNally
517 Terry McCann
518 Paul Byrne
519 Noel McGinn
520 Colm Donaghy

Footballers and Clubs – Monaghan

Answers on page 102

With which clubs would you associate the following Monaghan footballers?

521 Gerry McCarville
522 Eamon Murphy
523 Paddy Hamilton
524 Eamon McEneaney
525 Paddy Linden
526 Brendan Murray
527 Kevin Carragher
528 Ray McCarron
529 David Byrne
530 Ciaran Murray
531 Bernie Murray
532 Eugene Hughes
533 Fergus Caulfield

534 Michael O'Dowd
535 Declan Flanagan
536 Owen Hamilton
537 Declan Loughman
538 Gene Sherry
539 Gerry Hoey
540 P.J. Finlay

Footballers and Clubs – Mayo

Answers on page 103

With which clubs would you associate the following Mayo footballers?

541 Tom Reilly
542 Frank Noone
543 Anthony Finnerty
544 Gabriel Irwin
545 Willie Joe Padden
546 Joe Lindsay
547 John Finn
548 T.J. Kilgallon
549 Liam McHale
550 Sean Maher
551 Dermot Flanagan
552 Denis Kearney
553 Eugene Lavin
554 Martin Carney

555 Tom Morgan
556 Pat Holmes
557 Noel Durcan
558 Mark Butler
559 Michael Collins
560 Jimmy Burke

Footballers and Clubs – Cork

Answers on page 104

With which clubs would you associate the following Cork footballers?

561 John O'Driscoll
562 Shay Fahy
563 Larry Tompkins
564 Teddy McCarthy
565 Finbar Delaney
566 Tony Nation
567 Conor Counihan
568 Christy Ryan
569 Michael Slocum
570 Martin McCarthy
571 Tony Leahy
572 Colm O'Neill
573 Denis Walsh
574 Anthony Davis
575 Colman Corrigan

576 Paddy Hayes
577 Danny Culloty
578 John Kerins
579 John Cleary
580 Dave Barry

Footballers and Clubs – Meath

Answers on page 105

With which clubs would you associate the following Meath footballers?

581 Michael McQuillan
582 Mick Lyons
583 Liam Harnan
584 Liam Hayes
585 Robbie O'Malley
586 Padraic Lyons
587 Donal Smyth
588 Colm Coyle
589 Bernard Flynn
590 P.J. Gillic
591 Joe Cassels
592 Gerry McEntee
593 Frank Foley
594 Mattie McCabe
595 Brian Stafford
596 Colm O'Rourke

Friend or foe – action from the 1981 All-Ireland football final; Kerry v. Offaly

597 David Beggy
598 Terence Ferguson
599 Kevin Foley
600 Martin O'Connell

General Knowledge 11

Answers on page 106

601 Since 1900 only three counties have reached every Leinster senior football championship. Name them.
602 Up to 1988, when was the last time the Leinster final failed to produce a goal?
603 What about an Ulster final?
604 And Connacht?
605 Which two men share the distinction of having captained their counties to four All-Ireland finals?
606 One of the lowest-scoring All-Ireland senior football finals of all time was between Mayo and Kerry in 1906. What was the score?
607 When Galway beat Kerry in the 1964 senior football final, a tragedy for John Donnellan overshadowed the victory. What happened?
608 What delayed the playing of the 1956 Cork v. Galway football final?
609 Which was the first Ulster county to win an All-Ireland title?
610 In the 1928 Ulster football final between Armagh and Cavan held at Breifne Park why was play delayed?
611 Who won that final?
612 Who won the All-Ireland club football title on 17 March 1989?

613 Whom did they beat in the final?
614 Who won the All-Ireland club hurling title on the same day?
615 What was eventually postponed by the GAA at the end of March 1989?
616 Where is Nowlan Park?
617 Where is Pairc na nGael?
618 Where is St Molaise Park?
619 Where is Healy Park?
620 Where is Markievicz Park?

General Knowledge 12

Answers on page 107

621 Which county retained the All-Ireland senior football title with the same 15 players?
622 Name the Dublin player who survived a car crash to play again in an All-Ireland final.
623 In 1989 who were the Galway hurlers who announced they were emigrating?
624 Name the manager of the 1989 Derry football team.
625 In 1988 which county received the greatest number of All-Star awards in football?
626 How many counties were represented in the 1988 All-Star awards?
627 Name them.
628 In which years did Monaghan's Nudie Hughes win his first and second All-Star awards?
629 In 1989 Cork's Shay Fahy was unable to collect his All-Star award in person. Why?

630 Since 1971 which county has received the greatest number of All-Star awards?
631 How many – (a) 36; (b) 58; (c) 73 or (d) 91?
632 When was the London county board set up?
633 Up to 1988, how many times had London been All-Ireland junior football champions?
634 When did they first win the junior football title?
635 With which city would you associate Parnell Park?
636 What was Meath's first national title?
637 What was the purpose of the Croke Cup?
638 Who was the manager of the 1989 Dublin hurling team?
639 What did he win in 1958 and 1963?
640 What happened to him in 1961?

General Knowledge 13

Answers on page 108

641 Who was given a Bank of Ireland All-Time All-Star award in 1989?
642 Which Ulster side survived the quarter-finals of the National Football League in March 1989?
643 Whom did they beat?
644 Which other Ulster sides were beaten in those quarter-finals?
645 Who beat them?
646 What is unusual about the Roscommon club Ballaghaderreen?
647 In the 1988 All-Star hurling awards, which county achieved the greatest representation?

648 In the same year, which Wexford player was selected at midfield?
649 In the 1945 Railway Cup tournament two players faced each other in hurling and football on the same afternoon. Who were they?
650 Who was the first person to win Railway Cup hurling and football medals in the same year?
651 What position did he play?
652 Which was the first province to win four successive football titles?
653 In which years?
654 Two players were involved in all eight games. Who were they?
655 In which years did Ulster achieve their footballing four-in-a-row?
656 Who represented Ulster in all their eight games?
657 Which footballer scored four goals against Ulster in the 1975 Railway Cup?
658 In their world tour of Australia, New Zealand and the USA in 1970, Kerry played seven games. How many did they win?
659 Who was their top scorer on that tour?
660 Which county won the Dr McKenna Cup on 16 April 1989?

Minor Football

Answers on page 109

661 In the Leinster minor football championship, who have been Dublin's nearest rivals?
662 Which county won the first Ulster minor football championship in 1930?

663 Since then, which county has been the most successful in the championship?

664 Up to 1988, how many Ulster titles had they won?

665 Which county has never won an Ulster minor football title?

666 Who were the winners in the 1935 Ulster final, when Tyrone played Donegal?

667 Who won the first Connacht minor football title?

668 Which county won four successive Connacht minor football titles in the 1930s, 1960s and 1970s?

669 How often have Sligo been Connacht minor football champions?

670 After Mayo, which county is next in the order of merit?

671 Which three counties have never been on the losing side at the end of an All-Ireland minor football final?

672 When did Offaly win their first All-Ireland minor football title?

673 What was so remarkable about Kerry's 6–5 to 0–7 win over Mayo in the 1962 minor football final?

674 In which month was the 1951 Armagh v. Roscommon minor football final played?

675 Which province has held the All-Ireland minor football title for the longest period of time?

676 Up to 1988, when was the last occasion that the All-Ireland minor football final was contested by teams appearing for the first time?

677 Who is the only player to have captained minor and senior sides to All-Ireland wins?

678 What trophy is played for in the All-Ireland minor football championship?

679 Since Offaly's win in 1964, how many other Leinster counties have won the minor football championship?

680 Name the two team captains in the 1988 All-Ireland minor football final.

Camogie

Answers on page 110

681 When was the Camogie Association founded?

682 Where and when were the first inter-provincials staged?

683 In which year did Ulster first win the senior inter-provincial championships?

684 Which counties played in the first inter-county championship final in 1953?

685 When was the 'open draw' brought into the All-Ireland senior camogie championships?

686 In which year did teams from the same province contest the All-Ireland final?

687 Who were the winners and losers?

688 When was the junior championship introduced?

689 Who were the first winners?

690 What was unique about Patsy Rowan's display for Dublin Civil Service in a senior league match against Austin Stacks?

691 What was the score?

692 Who played in a junior and a senior final on the same day?

693 What record does Uña O'Connor hold?

694 Up to 1961, who had won 15 All-Ireland medals for Dublin?

695 Which team won the first All-Ireland club title?
696 Who were the losers in that final?
697 Which county has won the most titles in the National Senior League?
698 Up to 1988, how many titles had they won?
699 Which county won the National Junior League in 1988?
700 Up to 1988, name the counties that had won All-Ireland senior titles.

General Knowledge 14

Answers on page 112

701 Which member of the 1953 Armagh football team went on to become a well-known horse breeder?
702 In 1985, who took Monaghan into an All-Ireland semi-final replay with Kerry?
703 What position did Sean O'Neill play in when Down reached the 1960 and 1968 football finals?
704 Who was the outstanding scorer in the 1954 All-Ireland hurling semi-final between Wexford and Antrim?
705 Who was the first footballer to top the national scoring league with more than 100 points in one season?
706 Who broke the 100-point barrier in the following season?
707 Which Offaly player scored a personal best of 14 points in an All-Ireland football semi-final?
708 What was the year and who were Offaly's opponents?
709 Who was the first Carlow man to win an All-Ireland senior hurling medal?

710 In 1989, which counties reached the final of the National Hurling League?

711 Who were the beaten semi-finalists?

712 What were the scores in those semi-finals?

713 Whom did Tyrone beat in a play-off to reach Division Two of the National Football League in 1989?

714 Who won the 1989 'Home' National Football League final?

715 What was the score?

716 Who captained the Dublin team in that game?

717 In the same game, who played midfield for Dublin?

718 When did Cork last win the National Football League?

719 Which county has won the greatest number of National Football League titles?

720 Name the other county that is into double figures in league wins.

Hurlers and Clubs – Galway

Answers on page 113

With which clubs would you associate the following Galway hurlers?

721 Joe Cooney

722 John Commins

723 Conor Hayes

724 Ollie Kilkenny

725 Peter Finnerty

726 Ger McInerney

727 Seamus Coen
728 Steve Mahon
729 Pearse Piggot
730 Martin Naughton
731 Peter Murphy
732 Brendan Lynskey
733 Pakie Dervan
734 Tony Keady
735 Michael Coleman
736 Tony Cunningham
737 Michael Connolly
738 Noel Lane
739 Sylvie Linnane
740 Gerry Burke

Hurlers and Clubs – Cork

Answers on page 114

With which clubs would you associate the following Cork hurlers?

741 Ger Manley
742 Tony O'Sullivan
743 Kieran Kingston
744 Tomás Mulcahy
745 Pat Hartnett
746 John Fitzgibbon
747 Teddy McCarthy

Tony Doran of Buffers Alley bursting through the O'Donovan Rossa defence in the 1989 All-Ireland club hurling final.

748 Frank O'Sullivan
749 Ger Fitzgerald
750 John Meyler
751 Tom Cashman
752 Brian Cunningham
753 Denis Walsh
754 Jim Cashman
755 Richie Brown
756 John Crowley
757 Kevin Hennessy
758 Cathal Casey
759 John O'Callaghan
760 Denis Mulcahy

London Calling

Answers on page 115

London were All-Ireland junior football finalists in 1988. Match up these players with their counties of origin.

761 P.J. Burke
762 Joe Breen
763 Damien Carville
764 Richard Heraty
765 Martin Grant
766 Maurice Somers
767 Andy Hanley
768 Paul Dreelan

769 Tom Pidgeon
770 Richard Harnan
771 Ciaran White
772 Seamus Cassidy
773 Brendan Murphy
774 John Linden
775 Martin Hessian
776 Danny Duggan
777 Peter Reynolds
778 Pat Doyle
779 Who did London lose to in the 1988 junior football final?
780 What was the score?

General Knowledge 15

Answers on page 116

781 Who was charged with the murder of a fellow player in July 1929?
782 Who was the alleged victim?
783 Which county achieved the first treble in the All-Ireland hurling championship?
784 Which member of that team died in a training accident?
785 In the 1920s which hurler won two All-Ireland senior medals in the same year?
786 Galway's Leonard McGrath scored 3 goals in the 1923 hurling final. Where was he born?
787 Who were the winners of the 1989 Ulster under-21 football title?

788 In the final, who scored the winning goal that beat Down 1–6 to 1–5?

789 In April 1989 Rostrevor GAA Club opened a £250,000 complex. What is it called?

790 Name the 18-year-old who played in the 1988 All-Ireland senior hurling final.

791 When were the first Vocational Schools finals in football and hurling?

792 Who were the winners in the football competition that year?

793 Who were the first Ulster winners of the Vocational Schools football competition?

794 Name the 1989 football champions.

795 How many Vocational Schools football titles have Tyrone won?

796 Which other county shares the same number of titles with them?

797 Kilkenny were the losers of the first Vocational Schools hurling final. But who were the winners?

798 Antrim were the first Ulster side to win the Vocational Schools hurling title. In which year?

799 Which Vocational Schools side had an unbeaten run in hurling from 1980 to 1987?

800 When did Kilkenny win their first Vocational Schools hurling title?

Name the Grounds

Answers on page 117

What are the names of the Gaelic grounds in the following cities and towns?

801 Crossmaglen
802 Lurgan
803 Cootehill
804 Athy
805 Derry
806 Ballybofey
807 Newry
808 Ballinasloe
809 Newcastle, County Down
810 Castleblayney
811 Bagnalstown
812 Ballybay
813 Dungannon
814 Armagh
815 Portlaoise
816 Blackwatertown, County Armagh
817 Ballinascreen
818 Kingscourt
819 Carlow
820 Tubbercurry

Scribes and Commentators

Answers on page 118

With which newspapers or media forms would you associate the following Gaelic games journalists and broadcasters?

821 Kevin Cashman
822 Mick Dunne
823 Michael McGeary
824 Paddy Downey
825 Tony McGee
826 Michael Lyster
827 Peader O'Brien
828 Sean Kilfeather
829 David Walsh
830 John Campbell
831 Adrian Logan
832 Paddy O'Hara
833 Jerome Quinn
834 Jimmy Magee
835 Michael Ellard
836 Raymond Smith
837 Eamon O'Hara
838 Kevin Hughes
839 Jim O'Sullivan
840 Jackie Cummings

Referees of Yore

Answers on page 119

The following referees have taken charge of All-Ireland football finals over the years. Where are they from?

841 Harry Boland – 1914
842 Jim Byrne – 1930
843 Hugh Duggan – 1979
844 Pat Dunphy – 1915–19
845 Patsy Devlin – 1974
846 Willie Walsh – 1920–1
847 Seamus Alderidge – 1978
848 John McCarthy – 1903
849 Simon Deignan – 1958
850 Bill Delaney – 1946
851 Jim Flaherty – 1948
852 Fintan Tierney – 1972
853 Bill Goodison – 1955
854 Peter Waters – 1938
855 Tom Irwin – 1912
856 Tom Shelvlin – 1926–7
857 Peter McDermott – 1956
858 John Dunne – 1945
859 Paddy Mythen – 1946
860 John Moloney – 1973

Who Am I?

Answers on page 120

861 I was the oldest player on the field in the 1982 All-Ireland hurling final. Some would say that I'm the last line of defence. I won a Leinster minor medal in 1962. I'm a mechanic.

862 In two recent All-Ireland football finals I played in midfield. When I'm not actively involved in sport, I'm usually writing about it.

863 I made my senior hurling debut in 1980 and won a National Hurling League medal in 1982. I was 24 years old then and chairman of Glenmore Handball Club.

864 I made my third appearance in an All-Ireland final in 1987, when I was roving around the half-forward line. I'm used to taking orders as well as giving them. Ask anyone at Conahy Shamrocks!

865 I've been selected as an All-Star and I've won medals in hurling and football at minor, under-21 and senior levels. I was on the losing side in 1982. My job is to stop forwards and to catch criminals.

866 I first played hurling for my county in 1963. I lost my place but returned to win four National Hurling League medals. I will be remembered as the man who led the winning side in the first 80-minute final.

867 My club team is Birr. I captained my county minor football side when we won our first All-Ireland title at that level during the 1980s.

868 I've been a lifelong supporter of hurling. I was at one time hurling county secretary before becoming development officer for the sport in my province. I live on a peninsula.

Find the octopus — Oliver Murphy of Down in the tentacles of some Derry players in the 1986 Ulster minor football final.

869 It is said that I won four All-Ireland and six Leinster football medals without ever playing a match. But I wasn't always on the bench. I did play in the 1913 Leinster semi-final against Laois.

870 I won a minor football medal in the 1975 All-Ireland final. Since then my honours have included four Footballer of the Year awards. I'm a plumber.

871 My family roots are in Kerry, but I played my football north of the border. I was on a losing All-Ireland side in the 1970s. I'm a solicitor.

872 I lived and played in the Whitehall area of my native city and won my first All-Ireland senior football medal in 1976. I studied at Trinity College Dublin and I'm an engineer.

873 I'm equally at home on a hurling or football pitch, although I have to play for separate clubs, Ballycran and Carryduff. My father played football for Armagh. I'm a dentist.

874 In Gaelic football I'm a left fullback. At least that was my position in the 1981 All-Ireland final. We lost that one and I wasn't on the team the following year. I'm a carpenter.

875 I first played inter-county football in 1964, but then drifted out of the game for a while. In 1974 I made the first of five consecutive All-Ireland final appearances, playing at full-forward.

876 I was born in New York in the early 1950s, but the west of Ireland is now my home, where I'm involved in the hotel business. I played centre half-forward in the 1980 All-Ireland football final – we lost.

877 In 1974 I captained St Jarlaith's when we won the All-Ireland Colleges final. I led the county senior football team in 1980. We got out of Connacht in 1981. I'm a baker.

878 As team manager in 1979, I helped to guide my county to their first provincial final in 27 years. As a schoolboy, I played football for Ballyvourney College, Cork.

879 I played my football with Downings and played for my county when they took their first Ulster senior title in 1972. I made my county debut in 1969 and have won a couple of Dr McKenna Cup medals. I'm a teacher.

880 I was the first player from my club to be selected as county goalkeeper, but at St Ronan's I play outfield. In 1980 I conceded 3 goals to Armagh – but we beat them anyway.

Women Play Football Too

Answers on page 122

881 In which year was the Ladies Gaelic Football Association founded?

882 Is deliberate body contact permitted in the rules?

883 Can players pick the ball off the ground?

884 Who are the holders of the first All-Ireland senior championship?

885 Who were the beaten finalists?

886 Who captained Kerry in their 1987 All-Ireland win over Westmeath?

887 One Ulster team has taken the All-Ireland title. Which team and when?

888 Up to 1988, only one Connacht team had won the All-Ireland title. Which team and when?

889 When were the inter-provincial championships first staged?

890 Up to 1988, one province had never won the inter-provincial title. Which one?
891 Who were the first senior club champions in 1978?
892 Whom did they beat in the final?
893 In women's Gaelic football, how many points are awarded for a goal?
894 What size football is used in women's Gaelic football?
895 Up to 1988, how many counties had won the All-Ireland title?
896 Up to 1988, how many counties had been losers in the final?
897 That list of losers includes Cavan, Offaly, Roscommon and Tipperary. Name three other losers.
898 Which county has dominated women's Gaelic football since 1974?
899 In which year did the Ladies Gaelic Football Association start an under-18 championship?
900 In which county is the Watergrasshill club?

The American Scene

Answers on page 123

901 In which year were the New York championships established?
902 Which county took the inaugural hurling championship?
903 Up to 1988, which county had taken the greatest number of hurling titles?
904 How many – (a) 12; (b) 19; (c) 22 or (d) 30?
905 Which county won the 50th anniversary hurling championship in 1965?

906 Limerick have won the hurling title only once. When?
907 Until 1928, in which ground were the championship finals staged?
908 Which ground did they then move to?
909 What did this ground change its name to in 1945?
910 Which county won the first football championship in New York in 1915?
911 In which year did Gaelic Park, New York, start to host the finals?
912 Up to 1988, Cavan had won the football championship four times. When was the last time they won?
913 Which other Ulster counties can also lay claim to the title?
914 Which county had won the greatest number of football championships by the end of 1988?
915 When was the North American County Board given provincial status?
916 What had it previously been called?
917 Who were the winners of the first North American hurling and football championships in 1959?
918 Name the North American hurling and football champions of 1988.
919 Who were the first Canadian side to win a North American hurling title?
920 Who dominated the championships in hurling and football in 1983?

Name the Boss

Answers on page 124

Given the province and the year, name the winning Railway Cup football captains.

921 Connacht – 1937
922 Leinster – 1944
923 Ulster – 1964
924 Munster – 1949
925 Ulster – 1965
926 Leinster – 1945
927 Connacht – 1967
928 Leinster – 1988
929 Connacht – 1951
930 Munster – 1975

Given the province and the year, name the winning Railway Cup hurling captains.

931 Munster – 1946
932 Munster – 1958
933 Leinster – 1941
934 Connacht – 1982
935 Leinster – 1988
936 Leinster – 1962
937 Munster – 1976
938 Munster – 1937
939 Connacht – 1947
940 Leinster – 1967

True or False?

Answers on page 125

941 Michael Keating captained Tipperary to victory in the 1964 All-Ireland under-21 hurling championship.

942 Warwickshire's hurlers beat Kerry in the 1968 and 1969 All-Ireland junior finals.

943 Cork hold the most National Hurling League titles.

944 New York first competed in the National Hurling League finals in 1947–8.

945 Antrim beat Offaly to stay in Division One of the National Hurling League in 1989.

946 Liam McHale of Mayo is a first-class basketball player.

947 Monaghan's captain in the 1979 All-Ireland football semi-final against Kerry was Paddy Linden.

948 At that time both Linden and Brady played club football for Ballybay.

949 Roy McLarnen was manager of the Antrim under-21 football team that won the Ulster championship in 1989.

950 In Colleges hurling, St Flannan's of Ennis were the first winners of the Munster title in 1944.

951 Armagh's footballers have always played in saffron and white.

952 Dublin's Pat O'Neill is a veterinary surgeon.

953 Derry's Dermot McNicholl, now living in Australia, played club football for Glenullen.

954 Wicklow have a 100 per cent record of success in Leinster minor football finals.

955 Kildare are known as the 'Lilywhites'.

956 In the 1968 All-Ireland football final Sean O'Neill finished off a solo run from midfield by scoring a goal with a 20-yard shot.
957 Dublin's footballers changed to wearing dark blue shorts in 1974.
958 Armagh's reserve goalkeeper for the 1977 All-Ireland football final was Redmond Scullion of Pearse Ógs.
959 When the National Football League resumed after World War Two, Derry were the first Ulster winners.
960 Connacht's Railway Cup hurling side of 1982 was made up entirely of Galway players.

Handball

Answers on page 126

961 When was the Irish Handball Council established?
962 Which county was the famous John Joe Gilmartin from?
963 How many All-Ireland titles did he win during his career?
964 In which year did he win his first junior hardball singles title?
965 There was no softball championship in 1945. What was the reason?
966 When was the Gael Linn Cup introduced?
967 Who was its first winner?
968 What record did he equal in 1957?
969 RTE televised handball for the first time in 1973. What was the programme called?
970 Who were All-Ireland senior softball doubles champions in 1988?

971 Name the Limerick brothers who held the title in 1983, 1984 and 1986.
972 What was their other notable achievement in the 1980s?
973 Name the brothers who were hardball doubles champions in 1981 and 1982.
974 In 1988 which All-Ireland senior final did Tommie O'Rourke of Kildare lose?
975 Which All-Ireland senior title did O'Rourke win in 1988?
976 Where was his opponent, Peter McAuley, from?
977 Who won the world handball title for Ireland in the mid-1960s?
978 In pursuit of the title, where did he emigrate to in 1965?
979 On returning to Ireland, he continued to dominate the hardball and softball singles titles. What was his record?
980 What was significant about the All-Ireland senior softball singles title that Clare's Pat Kirby won in 1974?

General Knowledge 16

Answers on page 127

981 In which county would you find North Monastery College?
982 Whom did St Patrick's, Maghera, beat in a replay to win the 1989 Hogan Cup?
983 What was Cork's winning margin over New York in the first leg of the 1989 National Football League final?

984 Who scored Cork's goal in that first leg?
985 Who scored New York's goal?
986 Cork also won the second leg, but which player was left behind?
987 Which player suffered a ruptured Achilles tendon in the second leg of that final?
988 What colours do New York play in?
989 Which side shattered Burren's hopes of a seventh consecutive Down senior football title in 1989?
990 Who refereed the National Hurling League final in 1989?
991 Where were the 1988 world handball championships staged?
992 Pat Kirby won the masters singles final. Whom did he defeat?
993 In the 1988 American handball championships a Belfast woman took the softball title. Who is she and what club does she play with?
994 Which European country took an active interest in hurling in 1989?
995 Who were Connacht's representatives in the All-Ireland under-21 football championships in 1989?
996 Whom did they defeat in the All-Ireland semi-finals?
997 Padraig Dunne captained New York in the National Football League final against Cork in New York in May 1989. With which county had he previously won an All-Ireland senior medal?
998 Which well-known Roscommon player retired in 1989 after 17 years of inter-county football?

'It's mine,' says Tyrone's Frank McGuigan to Armagh's Denis Stevenson during the 1984 Ulster senior football final.

999 Who took the Man of the Match award in the 1988 National Hurling League final between Tipperary and Offaly?

1000 In which county would you find the women's Gaelic football team, St Monica's?

Answers

General Knowledge 1

Questions on page 3

1. Cork
2. 26
3. 1887
4. Mick O'Connell of Kerry in 1959
5. Kevin Moran
6. London
7. 1901
8. Larry Tompkins
9. Conor Hayes in 1987
10. Derry
11. Kilkenny
12. Kevin McCabe
13. Dave Barry of Cork
14. Dublin
15. Down
16. Dermot McNicholl
17. It was hurling's centenary year.
18. Gaelic Park, New York
19. Gerry McEntee of Meath
20. 1971

General Knowledge 2

Questions on page 4

21 John Dowling
22 None
23 No – nine members of the London team were expatriate Corkmen.
24 17
25 They did not score – 3–13 to 0–0
26 Eugene McKenna
27 Leixlip (Kildare)
28 Austin Stacks
29 Green for goals and white for points
30 Dan O'Keefe of Kerry
31 (a) 90,556
32 It was 1961 when Down beat Offaly; crowd capacity was subsequently reduced.
33 March 1979
34 Eight senior All-Ireland medals
35 John Doyle of Tipperary
36 Down
37 Paddy Doherty of Down – 1 goal 26 points
38 Brendan Mason of Down – 3 goals 18 points
39 1970
40 Kerry and Meath – Kerry were the winners.

General Knowledge 3

Questions on page 5

41 1975
42 Kerry and Dublin – Kerry were the winners.
43 Monaghan and Armagh
44 1972 – Offaly v. Kerry
45 Offaly – 1–19 to 0–13
46 1930, when they played Kerry
47 Tyrone
48 Cavan – they beat Galway in the 1933 final.
49 1928
50 Kildare – they beat Cavan.
51 Meath in 1988
52 In 1953 against Kerry and in 1977 against Dublin
53 Mayo
54 Michael, Pat and Tom
55 Tom
56 Tyrone's Frank McGuigan – he scored 11 points against Armagh.
57 Bookmaker Barney Eastwood – he played for Tyrone.
58 The Croke Park playing surface had been damaged during a U2 rock concert.
59 Tyrone – they played at Croke Park.
60 Seamus Darby; he scored a late winner against Kerry.

International Rules Football

Questions on page 7

61 Neil Kerley
62 80 minutes
63 6 points
64 3 points
65 A 'behind'
66 Pat Collins
67 Kevin Heffernan and Eugene McGee
68 Round
69 John O'Leary (Ireland) and Bruce Lindsay (Australia)
70 John Todd
71 Hawthorn in the Victoria Football League
72 1967, 1968 and 1984
73 The Australians did not play 'Ireland', but county sides – Meath and Mayo in 1967, Down, Kerry and a combined universities side in 1968.
74 New York – in 1967 they beat Australia in Gaelic Park.
75 Jet lag – they had played Mayo in Dublin the previous day (4 November 1967).
76 They won all their five games.
77 The Harry Beitzel Trophy, donated by the organiser of the 1967 tour.
78 *Footy Week*
79 Claremont, Western Australia
80 Ron Barassi

Hurling 1

Questions on page 8

81 John Fenton
82 Midleton
83 Tipperary captain Richard Stakelum, after the Munster hurling final
84 Teddy McCarthy and Denis Walsh
85 It is a competition where the winner is the person who can hurl a ball over a mountain course in the least number of strokes.
86 Cooley Mountain in County Louth
87 Ger Cunningham (Cork)
88 1923
89 1980
90 Cyril Farrell
91 The Liam McCarthy Cup
92 Galway (Meelick) and Tipperary (Thurles)
93 The Galway hurling team in 1932 – for leaving Mass early
94 1981 – they defeated Wexford 3–12 to 2–13
95 Limerick in 1897 and Offaly in 1981
96 Johnny Clifford
97 Loughgiel Shamrocks in 1983
98 St Rynagh's of Offaly – after a replay
99 38-year-old Tony Doran of Buffers Alley – he scored the winning goal.
100 Joe McKenna of Limerick

General Knowledge 4

Questions on page 9

101 Kildare
102 Five were for hurling (1941–4 and 1946), and one for football (1945).
103 Wexford – 1915–18
104 1929–32
105 Mayo – in the Connacht final
106 Cavan – they beat Kerry with a last-minute goal in the semi-final.
107 Johnny Riordan
108 They mimed some of the music.
109 Eoin Liston of Kerry
110 1913
111 Radio Éireann commentator Michael O'Hehir during the 1947 All-Ireland football final. He was asking for the transatlantic radio link to remain open.
112 Cavan v. Kerry at the Polo Grounds, New York.
113 Bill 'Squires' Gannon of Kildare in 1928
114 The Tipperary v. Dublin All-Ireland football final at Croke Park on 21 November 1920, when the Black and Tans opened fire on spectators and players.
115 15 people, 14 spectators and 1 player
116 Mick Hogan – Tipperary's right fullback
117 The Hogan Stand at Croke Park was named after him.
118 Their opponents Kerry considered not travelling to the match because of the death of their former captain, Dick Fitzgerald.
119 Mayo
120 1934, 1935, 1936, 1937, 1938 and 1939

Football 1

Questions on page 10

121 They were unbeaten in 57 matches.
122 Kerry claimed that the ball had hit a spectator before coming back into play.
123 Tommy Murphy, the Laois half-forward
124 He was 16 years old – against Offaly in 1937
125 August 1938
126 Four of the team were brothers – the Delaneys
127 He decided that Boylan had thrown the ball over the bar instead of punching it.
128 Tom O'Connor
129 In the 1937 All-Ireland senior replay, Kerry v. Cavan, as a substitute
130 Galway v. Cavan
131 It was played at Tuam; the ground could not cope with the large crowd that inched onto the playing pitch, causing endless delays.
132 Galway, and yes – Cavan's objections were overruled.
133 Eight
134 The referee blew for a foul, but the crowd thought the match was over and invaded the pitch. Most of the Kerry players had changed and left the ground before it was established that the final had not ended. The result was 2–4 to 0–7 in favour of Galway.
135 1940
136 County Carlow had been hit with foot-and-mouth disease and its team were not allowed to travel outside the county. Dublin were nominated for the semi-final.

137 Cork's Jack Lynch – he arrived at Croke Park just 15 minutes before the game against Cavan was due to start. All bus services to Croke Park had been delayed because of the crowds.

138 George Watterson

139 2–11 to 2–7

140 Philip

County Colours

Questions on page 13

141 White

142 Saffron

143 Blue with white collars

144 Green and white

145 White and red

146 Green and gold with white collars

147 Red with black collars

148 Gold and blue

149 Blue with yellow collars

150 Green, yellow and red

151 Maroon with white collars

152 Green and gold

153 Green and gold with white collars

154 Black and amber

155 Yellow with blue collars

156 White and black

157 Green with white collars

Kerry's majestic midfielder Mick O'Connell

158 Maroon with white collars
159 Blue and white
160 Red with white collars

General Knowledge 5

Questions on page 14

161 Cork refused to return to the field to play extra time.
162 The referee, Michael Greenan, threw in the ball. Barney Rock scored a goal and Dublin were declared the winners.
163 Danny Lynch
164 John Corvan
165 Armagh Harps
166 Ann Carroll
167 St Patrick's, Gleengoole-Ballingarry, Tipperary, in 1965 and St Paul's, Kilkenny, in 1968
168 Galway
169 They beat Tipperary – 2–16 to 4–8
170 Roscommon
171 Wrestling
172 Down 3–9, Derry 1–11
173 Casement Park, Belfast
174 Mickey Linden of Down
175 In respect for the 95 Liverpool spectators killed in the Hillsborough disaster at Sheffield the previous day (15 April 1989)
176 1958
177 Galway and Derry (football); Kilkenny and Clare (hurling)

178 1976
179 1973
180 Kerry (football) and Tipperary (hurling)

General Knowledge 6

Questions on page 15

181 They went to the dressing room and had showers.
182 Yes – Tipperary won.
183 Jimmy Barry-Murphy
184 Nemo Rangers
185 Antrim
186 Dinny Allen
187 Olcan McFetteridge of Antrim – he was playing for Armoy United.
188 Willie Bryan
189 Laois
190 Limerick
191 Kilkenny
192 Galway
193 Mayo
194 Kerry 2–5, Dublin 0–5
195 Tipperary – they were given a walkover against Limerick.
196 (d) 62
197 It was abandoned at half-time because a second ball was not available.
198 It was also abandoned at half-time because of a disagreement over the score.

199 Cork

200 Brian McCabe – he had played for Westmeath in the National Hurling League.

Clubs and Counties 1

Questions on page 16

201 Cork
202 Derry
203 Armagh
204 Dublin
205 Galway
206 Roscommon
207 Tyrone
208 Dublin
209 Down
210 Antrim
211 Kerry
212 Monaghan
213 Louth
214 Mayo
215 Limerick
216 Galway
217 Antrim
218 Monaghan
219 Armagh
220 Roscommon

General Knowledge 7

Questions on page 17

221 Buffers Alley
222 Tommy Guilfoyle
223 16 years
224 Babs Keating
225 The 'thunder and lightning' final
226 Because of the weather
227 Limerick and Kilkenny
228 Noel O'Dwyer
229 Bobby Ryan
230 Tipperary's County Board refused to toss for either Thurles or Cork.
231 The hay
232 Tipperary – they won the All-Ireland, the National League and the Oireachtas tournament.
233 Speed, style, skill, stamina and scoring
234 A racehorse
235 Niall Quinn – his father was Billy Quinn.
236 Martin Bailie of Down
237 Ballygalget
238 Borris-Ileigh
239 Clarecastle, Ballycastle, and Rathnure respectively
240 Kilruane McDonaghs

Footballers and Counties

Questions on page 19

241 Galway
242 Armagh
243 Fermanagh
244 Tyrone
245 Down
246 Cavan
247 Monaghan
248 Donegal
249 Tyrone
250 Derry
251 Offaly
252 Mayo
253 Dublin
254 Louth
255 Meath
256 Laois
257 Cork
258 Roscommon
259 Sligo
260 Kerry

Hurlers and Counties

Questions on page 20

261 Offaly
262 Antrim
263 Westmeath
264 Laois
265 Limerick
266 Clare
267 Kilkenny
268 Wexford
269 Tipperary
270 Galway
271 Down
272 Offaly
273 Antrim
274 Galway
275 Armagh
276 Kilkenny
277 Armagh
278 Limerick
279 Kilkenny
280 Cork

Clubs and Counties 2

Questions on page 22

281 Offaly
282 Cork
283 Wexford
284 Cork
285 Kilkenny
286 Cork
287 Antrim
288 Kilkenny
289 Kilkenny
290 Galway
291 Down
292 Waterford
293 Down
294 Derry
295 Armagh
296 Tipperary
297 Down
298 Antrim
299 Tipperary
300 Wexford

Brothers

Questions on page 23

301 Five
302 Four brothers and an uncle
303 Tom
304 John, Joe and Michael Connolly
305 Bobby, Billy and Nicky Rackard
306 Ger, Liam, Sean and Kevin Fennelly
307 Dan, Martin, John and Pat Quigley
308 1962 – Kerry beat Roscommon
309 Sean Óg, Niall and Paudie Sheehy
310 Tralee
311 John Joe Sheehy was a selector.
312 Tim, John Joe and Bill Landers (Bill was a substitute)
313 Spillane
314 Ger and Brian Cunningham
315 Tom, John and Pat O'Connor
316 Noel, Jimmy and Vincent Lucey
317 Cavan
318 Liam and Matt Connor
319 Tommy, Vincent and Brendan McGovern
320 The McManuses

Football 2

Questions on page 24

321 1942 – they beat Munster 1–10 to 1–5.
322 Kevin Armstrong of Antrim – the score was 1–6 to 0–3.
323 Cavan, with seven players
324 Derry, Down and Fermanagh
325 Meath
326 1949 – they beat Cavan 1–10 to 1–6.
327 Brian Smyth and Mick O'Brien – they were in the dressing room deciding which of them would captain the team.
328 Brian Smyth
329 Bill McCorry
330 The Kerry goalkeeper picked the ball off the ground inside the square.
331 Kerry beat them 0–13 to 1–6.
332 They beat Cavan at Casement Park.
333 The other 14 Dublin players were from St Vincent's – O'Grady played with the Air Corps.
334 He was the first Cahirciveen club man to play on a winning Kerry side.
335 Jack Murphy
336 Kevin Heffernan
337 Limerick
338 Louth captain Dermot O'Brien – he was late for the game.
339 A showband
340 'The Merry Ploughboy' in 1966

Lavey's Henry Downey fastest of all in escaping the tackle from Rossa's Donal Armstrong during the 1988 Ulster club hurling final.

Hurling 2

Questions on page 26

341 Pat Carroll, who died in March 1986 – he had played against Antrim in the semi-final.
342 Tom Cashman
343 Pat Henderson
344 Red with white collars
345 Blue and gold
346 White with blue collars
347 Purple and yellow
348 Ken Hogan
349 Against Clare in the Munster semi-final
350 Wexford
351 Dublin, at Casement Park
352 Jimmy Langton of Kilkenny
353 In 1940 against Limerick, and Kilkenny were beaten 3–7 to 1–7.
354 Kevin Hennessy
355 1959
356 10 years
357 Offaly
358 O'Donovan Rossas
359 Lavey
360 Richard Stakelum (Tipperary) and Kevin Hennessy (Cork)

Football 3

Questions on page 27

361 Sean Cunningham – the score was 1–9 to 1–7.
362 Offaly
363 Johnny Culloty – Kerry's goalkeeper
364 Paddy Doherty
365 1964, 1965, and 1966
366 John Donnellan
367 None
368 Anton O'Toole
369 Thirteen in a row
370 Eight – 1975–82
371 Ambrose O'Donovan
372 Gneeveguilla
373 A boat
374 They lived on Valentia Island, off Kerry's south-west coast. A bridge now links the island to the mainland.
375 Tredaghs were awarded a walkover.
376 Dublin – because a goal outweighed any number of points scored.
377 A draw – a goal equalled 5 points.
378 Jack O'Shea of Kerry
379 Four
380 1980, 1981, 1984 and 1985

General Knowledge 8

Questions on page 28

381 Maurice Davin of Tipperary
382 Paddy Buggy of Kilkenny
383 Padraig McNamee of Antrim (1938–43)
384 20 years – from 1901 to 1921, when Daniel McCarthy of Dublin succeeded James Nowlan of Kilkenny
385 Four
386 Padraig McNamee of Antrim, 1938–43; Seamus McFerran of Belfast, 1955–8; Alf Murray of Armagh, 1964–7; and Paddy McFlynn of Down, 1979–82.
387 Thurles
388 Dublin
389 Fitzgerald Stadium
390 1958
391 Jim McKeever of Derry
392 Two
393 Jim McCartan of Down in 1961 and 1962 and Sean O'Neill of Down in 1968
394 Kevin Heffernan of Dublin in 1974
395 Tony Wall of Tipperary in 1958
396 In Hayes Hotel, Thurles, on 1 November 1884
397 Dr Thomas William Croke, Archbishop of Cashel, who gave the GAA his blessing when it was formed in 1884.
398 Michael Cusack, one of the founders of the GAA
399 1981
400 Galway

Referees do have Homes!

Questions on page 29

401 Down
402 Kildare
403 Antrim
404 Sligo
405 Kilkenny
406 Clare
407 Roscommon
408 Kerry
409 Derry
410 Tipperary
411 Laois
412 Antrim
413 Kildare
414 Westmeath
415 Kerry
416 Waterford
417 Sligo
418 Cork
419 Fermanagh
420 Meath

General Knowledge 9

Questions on page 30

421 University College Cork
422 St Mary's College, Belfast
423 They beat University College Cork, 3–13 to 1–5.
424 Maurice Fitzgerald
425 University College Galway
426 University of Ulster at Jordanstown, 1–8 to 1–6
427 Trinity College Dublin and Queen's University Belfast
428 St Patrick's, Maghera, and St Colman's, Newry
429 St Patrick's
430 Adrian McGuckan
431 St Patrick's and St Colman's
432 St Colman's
433 The Hogan Cup
434 Mícheál Ó Muircheartaigh
435 Eamon Grieve
436 Gabriel Kelly
437 Peter Quinn
438 Father Dan Gallogly of Cavan
439 Gene Larkin of Armagh
440 Cavan

Minor Gaelic Games

Questions on page 32

441 Clare
442 1929
443 Tipperary in 1934 – there had been a dispute over the Dublin v. Tyrone semi-final and Tipperary were declared winners.
444 15
445 Dublin and Kerry – they have both won 10.
446 Once
447 In 1970, Galway v. Kerry
448 Galway
449 Five
450 Armagh, Cavan, Derry, Down and Tyrone
451 Monaghan, in 1939
452 Kerry
453 Cork
454 1985, 1986 and 1987
455 Three
456 1949, 1951 and 1957
457 Kerry
458 Longford
459 Dublin
460 Yes, once – in 1938 when they beat Louth

General Knowledge 10

Questions on page 34

461 Kevin Heffernan
462 The city arms crest
463 Denis
464 Thurles
465 New York
466 Casement Park, Belfast
467 St Tiernach's Park, Clones
468 Cork
469 Patrickswell and Mount Sion
470 Patrickswell
471 Buffers Alley and St Rynagh's
472 Ciaran Barr
473 O'Donovan Rossas
474 Two – they were beaten by Dublin in 1976 and Offaly in 1982.
475 1985
476 Kerry v. Monaghan and Dublin v. Mayo
477 University of Ulster at Jordanstown
478 University College Galway
479 Enniskillen
480 Wexford

Football 4

Questions on page 35

481 Galway
482 37
483 1905 – they beat Mayo.
484 1977, 1978, 1979 and 1980
485 Roscommon 0–2, Galway 0–0
486 1975 – they beat Mayo in a replay.
487 Fermanagh
488 41 years – they last won in 1938.
489 1888, when Monaghan won
490 1890
491 1969
492 Derry in 1976
493 Kilkenny, in 1888
494 1944
495 Dublin
496 1945
497 1939 – they beat Wexford.
498 1965 and 1968
499 They lost to Dublin in 1965 and beat Laois in 1968.
500 38

Footballers and Clubs – Tyrone

Questions on page 36

501 Drumquin
502 Trillick
503 Carrickmore
504 Castlederg
505 Aghyaran
506 Moy
507 Clonoe
508 Ballygawley
509 Augher
510 Aughabrack
511 Omagh
512 Pomeroy
513 Newtownstewart
514 Coalisland
515 Cookstown
516 Brackaville
517 Killyclogher
518 Aghyaran
519 Killyclogher
520 Moy

Down forward Brendan Mason loses possession to Meath defender Kevin Foley.

Footballers and Clubs – Monaghan

Questions on page 37

521 Scotstown
522 Emyvale
523 Latton
524 Castleblayney
525 Ballybay
526 Clones
527 Clontibret
528 Scotstown
529 Garda, Dublin
530 Parnells
531 Scotstown
532 Castleblayney
533 Scotstown
534 Clontibret
535 Castleblayney
536 Latton
537 Castleblayney
538 Scotstown
539 Inniskeen
540 Ballybay

Footballers and Clubs – Mayo

Questions on page 38

541 Castlebar Mitchels
542 Hollymount
543 Moygownagh
544 Glenaboy
545 Belmullet
546 Kiltane
547 Mayo Gaels
548 Balla
549 Ballina Stephenites
550 Civil Service, Dublin
551 Civil Service, Dublin
552 Swinford
553 Kiltimagh
554 Castlebar Mitchels
555 Ballaghaderreen
556 Moy
557 Ballaghaderreen
558 Kilmaine
559 Lacken
560 Aughamore

Footballers and Clubs – Cork

Questions on page 39

561 Ballingeary
562 Nemo Rangers
563 Castlehaven
564 Glanmire
565 St Michael's
566 Nemo Rangers
567 Aghada
568 St Finbarr's
569 St Finbarr's
570 Youghal
571 St Finbarr's
572 Midleton
573 St Catherine's
574 O'Donovan Rossas
575 Macroom
576 St Finbarr's
577 Newmarket
578 St Finbarr's
579 Castlehaven
580 Nemo Rangers

Footballers and Clubs – Meath

Questions on page 40

581 St Patrick's
582 Summerhill
583 Moynalvey
584 Skryne
585 St Colmcille's
586 Summerhill
587 Navan O'Mahonys
588 Seneschalstown
589 St Colmcille's
590 Carnaross
591 Navan O'Mahonys
592 Nobber
593 Trim
594 Seneschalstown
595 Kilmainhamwood
596 Skryne
597 Navan O'Mahonys
598 Gaeil Colmcille
599 Trim
600 St Michael's

General Knowledge 11

Questions on page 42

601 Kildare, Louth and Meath
602 1986 – Meath 0–9, Dublin 0–7
603 1987 – Derry 0–11, Armagh 0–9
604 1987 – Galway 0–8, Mayo 0–7
605 Footballers Sean Kennedy of Wexford, 1913–17, and Tony Hanahoe of Dublin, 1976–9
606 Mayo 0–1, Kerry 0–1
607 During the game, his father died in the Hogan Stand.
608 There was a polio epidemic in County Cork – the game was eventually played in October.
609 Armagh – they were junior football champions in 1926.
610 The ball had been kicked into a field of oats and took some time to find.
611 Cavan – they beat Armagh 2–6 to 1–4.
612 Nemo Rangers
613 Clann na Gael (Roscommon)
614 Buffers Alley – they beat O'Donovan Rossas.
615 The 1989 International Rules tour of Australia by Ireland
616 Kilkenny
617 Limerick
618 Irvinestown
619 Omagh
620 Sligo

General Knowledge 12

Questions on page 43

621 Kildare, in 1927 and 1928
622 Brian Mullins
623 Tony Keady and Brendan Lynskey
624 Tommy Diamond
625 Meath – with five players
626 Five
627 Cork, Dublin, Kerry, Meath and Monaghan
628 1979 and 1985
629 He was serving with the UN peace-keeping force in Lebanon.
630 Kerry
631 (c) 73
632 1896
633 Six times
634 1938
635 Dublin
636 They won the Croke Cup (for football) in 1911, when they beat Waterford in the final.
637 For the runners-up in the provincial finals
638 Lar Foley
639 All-Ireland football medals with Dublin
640 He was sent off in the All-Ireland hurling final against Tipperary.

General Knowledge 13

Questions on page 44

641 Kevin Armstrong of Antrim
642 Cavan
643 Derry
644 Armagh and Antrim
645 Cork beat Armagh and Kerry beat Antrim.
646 They play in the Mayo league.
647 Galway, with seven players
648 George O'Connor
649 Kevin Armstrong of Ulster and Jack Lynch of Munster
650 Des Foley of Leinster in 1962
651 Midfield
652 Leinster
653 1952, 1953, 1954 and 1955
654 Stephen White of Louth and Ollie Freeney of Dublin
655 1963, 1964, 1965 and 1966
656 Paddy Doherty of Down
657 Jimmy Barry-Murphy of Cork and Munster
658 All seven
659 Mick O'Dwyer – 9 goals 30 points
660 Down – they beat Derry.

Minor Football

Questions on page 45

661 Louth – they have taken 8 provincial titles to Dublin's 24.
662 Armagh
663 Tyrone
664 13
665 Fermanagh
666 Neither team won – there were objections from both sides and the game was declared null and void.
667 Mayo in 1930
668 Mayo – 1933–6, 1961–4 and 1977–80
669 Twice – in 1949, after an objection against Roscommon, and in 1968, when they beat Galway.
670 Galway
671 Roscommon, Galway and Offaly
672 1964 – they beat Cork.
673 It was the first time that six goals were scored in the second half of a final.
674 December – there had been delays in deciding the Connacht championship.
675 Leinster – Dublin and Meath were winners for six years in a row, 1954–9.
676 1939 – Monaghan v. Roscommon
677 Dublin's Des Foley in 1958 and 1963
678 The Markham Cup
679 One – Dublin in 1979, 1982 and 1984
680 Danny Cahill of Kerry and Gearóid O'Regan of Dublin

Camogie

Questions on page 47

681　1904
682　Navan in 1954
683　1967
684　Dublin beat Galway, 3–2 to 0–2
685　1973
686　1976
687　Kilkenny beat Galway
688　1968
689　Down
690　She was the only scorer.
691　7 goals 1 point
692　Cally Riordan of Cork in 1973
693　She won her tenth successive All-Ireland senior medal with Dublin in 1966.
694　Kathleen Mills, between 1942 and 1961
695　Celtic of Dublin in 1964
696　Deirdre of Antrim
697　Kilkenny
698　Six
699　Armagh – they beat Dublin.
700　Antrim, Cork, Dublin, Kilkenny and Wexford

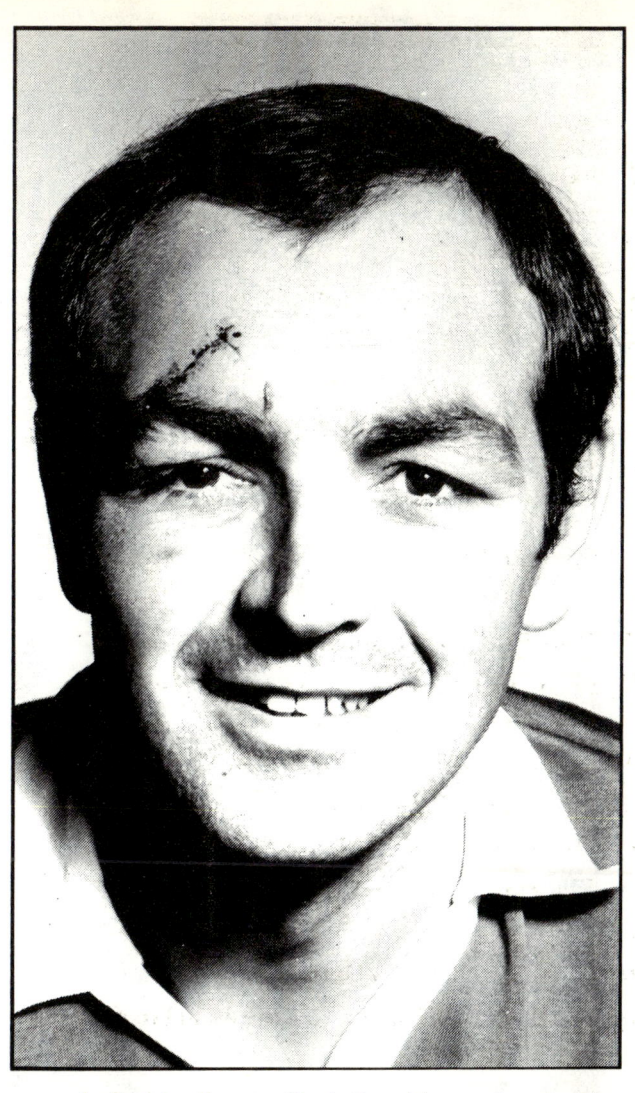

War wound – Cork hurling star Denis Coughlan carries a battle scar.

General Knowledge 14

Questions on page 48

701 Frank Kernan
702 Eamon McEneaney – he scored an equalising point in injury time.
703 Right half-forward in 1960 and full-forward in 1968
704 Nicky Rackard – he scored 7 goals 7 points.
705 Frank Donnelly of Tyrone in 1956, with 106 points
706 Frank Donnelly again, with 117 points
707 Tony McTeague
708 1972 against Donegal
709 Mick Morrissey of Ballycrinnegan – he played left half-back for Wexford against Galway in 1955.
710 Galway and Tipperary
711 Dublin and Kilkenny
712 Tipperary 0–15, Kilkenny 1–11; Galway 2–13, Dublin 1–9
713 Limerick – the score was 1–7 to 1–6.
714 Cork
715 Cork 0–15, Dublin 0–12
716 Gerry Hargan
717 Jim Ronayne and Paul Bealin
718 1980 – they beat Kerry.
719 Kerry, with 14 titles
720 Mayo, with 10 titles

Hurlers and Clubs – Galway

Questions on page 49

721 Sarsfields
722 Gort
723 Kiltomer
724 Kiltomer
725 Mullagh
726 Kinvara
727 Mullagh
728 Beagh
729 Gort
730 Turloughmore
731 Loughrea
732 Meelick Eyrecourt
733 Kiltomer
734 Killmordaly
735 Abbeyknockmoy
736 St Thomas's
737 Castlegar
738 Ballindereen
739 Gort
740 Turloughmore

Hurlers and Clubs – Cork

Questions on page 50

741 Inniscarra
742 Na Piarsaigh
743 Tracton
744 Glen Rovers
745 Midleton
746 Glen Rovers
747 Sarsfields
748 Glen Rovers
749 Midleton
750 St Finbarr's
751 Blackrock
752 St Finbarr's
753 St Catherine's
754 Blackrock
755 Blackrock
756 Bishopstown
757 Midleton
758 St Catherine's
759 Ballyhea
760 Midleton

London Calling

Questions on page 52

761 Mayo
762 Cork
763 Down
764 Mayo
765 Donegal
766 Down
767 Mayo
768 Wexford
769 Mayo
770 Sligo
771 Cork
772 Mayo
773 Sligo
774 Down
775 Galway
776 Derry
777 Leitrim
778 Kildare
779 Mayo
780 1–10 to 0–3

General Knowledge 15

Questions on page 53

781 Jim Smith of Cavan
782 Armagh's Jamesy Kernan – he died following a collison in the Ulster football final.
783 Cork, in 1892, 1893 and 1894
784 Willie John O'Connell – he was hit accidentally by a hurley.
785 Mick Gill; he played full-forward for Galway in the 1923 final – played in September 1924; two months later he played for Dublin in the 1924 final.
786 Australia
787 Antrim
788 Chris Murphy
789 St Bronagh's
790 John Leahy – Tipperary's right half-forward
791 1961
792 Cork City – they beat Offaly.
793 Fermanagh in 1966
794 Tyrone
795 Five
796 Kerry
797 Limerick City, in 1961
798 1971
799 Galway
800 1963 – they defeated Cork City.

Name the Grounds

Questions on page 55

801 St Oliver Plunkett Park
802 Davitt Park
803 Hugh O'Reilly Park
804 Geraldine Park
805 Celtic Park
806 Seán Mac Cumhaill Park
807 Pairc an Iúir
808 Duggan Park
809 St Patrick's Park
810 St Mary's Park
811 McGrath Park
812 Pearse Park
813 O'Neill Park
814 Athletic Grounds
815 O'Moore Park
816 O'Neill Park
817 Dean McGlinchey Park
818 Father Murray Park
819 Dr Cullen Park
820 Kilcoyne Park

Scribes and Commentators

Questions on page 56

821 *Sunday Tribune*
822 RTE
823 *Sunday Life*
824 *Irish Times*
825 *Irish News*
826 RTE
827 *Irish Press*
828 *Irish Times*
829 *Sunday Tribune*
830 *Belfast Telegraph*
831 UTV
832 BBC
833 BBC
834 RTE
835 *Cork Examiner*
836 *Sunday Independent*
837 *News Letter*
838 *Sunday World*
839 *Cork Examiner*
840 BBC

Referees of Yore

Questions on page 57

841 Dublin
842 Wexford
843 Armagh
844 Laois
845 Tyrone
846 Waterford
847 Kildare
848 Kilkenny
849 Cavan
850 Laois
851 Offaly
852 Cavan
853 Wexford
854 Kildare
855 Cork
856 Roscommon
857 Meath
858 Galway
859 Wexford
860 Tipperary

Who Am I?

Questions on page 58

861 Noel Skehan of Kilkenny
862 Liam Hayes of Meath
863 Christy Heffernan of Kilkenny
864 Kieran Brennan of Kilkenny – an officer in the Irish Army
865 Brian Murphy of Cork – a Garda
866 Paddy Barry of Cork – the first 80-minute final was in 1970.
867 Michael Hogan – Offaly captain against Cork in 1986
868 Seamus McGratton of Down
869 Barney Roice of Wexford
870 Jack O'Shea of Kerry
871 Paddy Moriarty of Armagh
872 Tommy Drumm of Dublin
873 Greg Blaney of Down
874 Charlie Conroy of Offaly
875 Jimmy Keaveney of Dublin
876 John O'Gara of Roscommon
877 Henry Gavin
878 Sean McCague of Monaghan
879 Hugh McClafferty of Donegal
880 Gay Sheerin of Roscommon

'Can I have this dance?' – a question for Cork's Niall Cahalane from Meath forward Bernie Flynn during the 1988 All-Ireland football final.

Women Play Football Too

Questions on page 61

881 1974, in Thurles
882 No
883 Yes – provided they are in a standing position
884 Tipperary in 1974
885 Offaly
886 Margaret Flaherty
887 Cavan in 1977 – they beat Roscommon.
888 Roscommon in 1978
889 1976
890 Ulster
891 Mullahoran of Cavan
892 Newtownshandrum of Cork
893 3 points
894 Size four
895 Five – Cavan, Kerry, Offaly, Roscommon and Tipperary
896 Nine
897 Galway, Laois, Leitrim, Westmeath and Wexford
898 Kerry, with seven in a row – 1982 to 1988
899 1980
900 Cork

The American Scene

Questions on page 62

901 1915
902 Galway
903 Tipperary
904 (b) 19
905 Galway
906 1961
907 Celtic Park
908 Inisfail Park
909 Croke Park
910 Cavan
911 1952
912 1984
913 Donegal, Fermanagh, Monaghan and Tyrone
914 Kerry, with 21
915 1950
916 The Midwestern State League
917 Hurling – San Francisco; football – Los Angeles
918 Hurling – San Francisco Gaels; football – Chicago Wolfe Tones
919 Montreal in 1961
920 Hurling – Chicago Harry Bolands; football – St Brendan's

Name the Boss

Questions on page 64

921 Purty Kelly of Mayo
922 Jim Thornton of Louth
923 Paddy Doherty of Down
924 Batt Garvey of Kerry
925 Charlie Gallagher of Cavan
926 Peeny Whelan of Carlow
927 Enda Colleran of Galway
928 Michael McQuillan of Meath
929 Sean Flanagan of Mayo
930 Billy Morgan of Cork
931 Christy Ring of Cork
932 Phil Grimes of Waterford
933 Bobby Hinks of Kilkenny
934 Sean Silke of Galway
935 Aidan Fogarty of Offaly
936 Noel Dromgoole of Dublin
937 Eamon O'Donoghue of Cork
938 Mick Mackey of Limerick
939 Sean Duggan of Galway
940 Ollie Walsh of Kilkenny

True or False?

Questions on page 65

941 False – Owen Killoran was captain.
942 True
943 False – Tipperary hold the most with 15 to Cork's 12.
944 False – it was 1949–50.
945 True
946 True
947 False – it was Brendan Brady.
948 False – Brady played for Parnells in Dublin.
949 True
950 True
951 False – until the mid-1920s they played in Kilkenny's colours, black and amber.
952 False – he is a medical doctor.
953 True
954 True – they only played once, in 1974 when they beat Longford.
955 True
956 False – he scored when Peter Rooney's shot came off the Kerry post.
957 True
958 False – it was Malachy Heaney
959 True – they defeated Clare in the 1946–7 final.
960 False – two players were from Mayo.

Handball

Questions on page 66

961 1924
962 Kilkenny
963 25
964 1935
965 There was a shortage of rubber.
966 1954
967 John Ryan of Wexford
968 John Joe Gilmartin's 1939 record, when he won all four All-Ireland handball titles available to him.
969 *Top Ace*
970 Michael Walsh and Eugene Downey of Kilkenny
971 John and Tom Quish
972 They were four-times All-Ireland hardball doubles champions from 1984 to 1987.
973 Cecil and Pius Winders from Kildare
974 He lost in the Coca-Cola singles final to Kilkenny's Michael Walsh.
975 The senior hardball singles title
976 Louth
977 Joe Maher
978 Toronto, Canada
979 He won both titles in 1968, 1969 and 1970, and the softball title again in 1973.
980 It was first time that the championship was 'open draw'.

General Knowledge 16

Questions on page 67

981 Cork
982 Coláiste Chríost Rí from Cork
983 7 points – the score was 1–12 to 1–5
984 John Cleary
985 J.P. O'Kane
986 Teddy McCarthy – he missed the team bus to Gaelic Park.
987 Cork defender Colman Corrigan
988 White jerseys with blue cuffs, and blue shorts
989 Clonduff – they beat Burren 1–9 to 1–6.
990 John Denton of Wexford
991 Melbourne, Australia
992 His brother, John
993 Una Mulgrew from St Paul's, Belfast
994 The Netherlands – they wanted to stage a tournament in Amsterdam.
995 Galway
996 Meath
997 Offaly in 1982
998 Harry Keegan
999 John Kennedy of Tipperary
1000 Dublin

OTHER TITLES
from
THE BLACKSTAFF PRESS

BELFAST CELTIC
MARK TUOHY

The legendary Belfast Celtic Football Club flourished from 1891 to 1949, attracting enthusiasm and admiration from the sporting community. During that time, the team were Irish League Champions fourteen times, Irish Cup Winners eight times, City Cup Winners ten times, Gold Cup Winners seven times – the list goes on and on. Many of its stars – Keiller McCullough, Charlie Tully, Boy Martin – went on to play for famous English teams; many will remember Jackie Vernon's fine record with West Bromwich Albion. The team was founded in emulation of Glasgow Celtic, and there were always close links between the players and supporters of the two clubs.

This vivid illustrated account of the triumphs and disappointments of a great Irish team is based on Club records, newspaper files and, most importantly, on the memories of old players and supporters.

198 x 129 mm; 96 pp; 0 85640 139 0; pb

£4.50

THE BOOK OF THE IRISH COUNTRYSIDE

The Book of the Irish Countryside is a richly illustrated treasury of information on the island of Ireland: its landforms and weather patterns, landscapes and scenery, trees and plants; its natural environment as habitat for birds, fish and mammals; and the complex interaction between land and people.

Geologists and geographers, naturalists and historians, archaeologists, explorers, folklorists and environmentalists have all contributed to this busy and challenging book. They examine the surprising diversity of the island's weather and natural features – from wetlands, mountains and peatlands to woods, caves, limestone pavements and drumlins. They discuss how animal and plant life first reached Ireland and how it is surviving the onslaughts of twentieth-century urbanisation, pollution and farming methods. There are articles on forestry, waterways, ancient monuments, thatched cottages and much more.

The writers have in common a heartfelt desire to save Ireland's natural richness from further destruction. They urge their readers to learn, discover, enjoy and preserve...

230 x 242 mm; 288 pp; 0 85640 384 9; hb

£12.95

IF EVER YOU GO TO DUBLIN TOWN
A HISTORIC GUIDE TO THE CITY'S STREET NAMES
CAROL AND JONATHAN BARDON

The heart of Dublin is lively and bustling, welcoming citizen and tourist alike with its friendly pubs, fashionable shops, hawkers' stalls and up-market restaurants. But the contrasting faces of the city – modernistic office blocks, gracious Georgian houses, crumbling tenements – hint at its fascinating history.

Street names, strange in a modern context, lead us into the past – Bull Alley, Weaver's Square, Golden Lane, Mary's Abbey, Fishamble Street. The unremarkable Hammond Lane takes on a sinister glamour when we discover it was originally Hangman's Lane. Names from the days of British domination like Grafton, Capel and Camden jostle indiscriminately with those of great Irish patriots like Sean Mac Dermott, Lord Edward and Cathal Brugha. And some names, such as Wood Quay, have their origins in the early infancy of the city.

Attractively illustrated, this excellent new pocket guide explains the names of over two hundred of the most historic and interesting streets, transforming a casual stroll around the city into an exciting time voyage back to its tumultuous past.

180 x 107 mm; 128 pp; 0 85640 397 0; pb

£3.50 stg, IR£3.95

THE BOOK OF
ULSTER SURNAMES
ROBERT BELL

What's your name? What was your mother called? And her mother? What was your father's mother's name? Most of us know at least a few of the surnames that make up the heritage of our own families. But what do these names mean and where did they come from?

The Book of Ulster Surnames has entries for over five hundred of the most common family names of the province, with references to thousands more, and is packed with unexpected insights into the complex, turbulent origins of the Ulster people.

'... the most interesting book I have come across in a long time... Fascinating, fascinating, fascinating: buy yourself a late Christmas present, and have hours of entertainment.'
Kevin Myers, *Irish Times*

198 x 129 mm; 304 pp; 0 85640 416 0; hb
£12.95
0 85640 405 5; pb
£6.95

ORDERING BLACKSTAFF BOOKS

All Blackstaff Press books are available through bookshops. In the case of difficulty, however, orders can be made directly to the publisher. Indicate clearly the title and number of copies required and send order with your name and address to:

**Cash Sales
Blackstaff Press Limited
3 Galway Park
Dundonald
Belfast BT16 0AN
Northern Ireland**

Please enclose a remittance to the value of the cover price plus: 60p for the first book plus 30p per copy for each additional book ordered to cover postage and packing. Payment should be made in sterling by UK personal cheque, postal order, sterling draft or international money order, made payable to Blackstaff Press Limited.

Applicable only in the UK and Republic of Ireland
Full catalogue available on request